D1408555

MY TURN BIBLE STORIES ABOUT
ABCs

Sarah Fletcher

Illustrated by Joe VanSeveren

CPH
SAINT LOUIS

Copyright © 1999 Concordia Publishing House

3558 S. Jefferson Avenue, St. Louis, MO 63118-3968

Manufactured in the United States of America

1   2   3   4   5   6   7   8   9   10   08   07   06   05   04   03   02   01   00   99

This book belongs to

....

Aa

A is for **all** things.

Apricots and ants, acorns and asteroids, Aprils and Airedales, and afternoons.

God made **all** things.

Aa

Praise God for
the **A** things.
ALLELUIA!

5

Bb

B is for **big bears** and **baby bears** too.

God made **bears** and **bugs** and **birthdays**. Praise God for the **B** things.

6

C is for **cats** and **cream**.

Cc

And **canaries** safe in their **cages**. Praise God for the **C** things.

7

Dd

D is for the **dogs** God made.

And **daylight**
and **daisies**.
Praise God for
the **D** things.

8

E is for **EEK!** God made **elephants**.

And **evening**
and **Easter**
and **everyone**
you know.
Praise God for
the **E** things.

Ff

F is for **fish** and **feet** and **fathers**.

And **Fridays** and **France** and **fun** with your **friends**. Praise God for the **F** things.

G is for **grandmas** and **grandpas** and **geese**.

Gg

And **gardens** and **giggles** and **golden** retrievers. Praise God for the **G** things.

Hh

H is for **hamsters**.

And **hedgehogs**
and **honey**
and **hearts**
full of love.
Praise God for
the **H** things.

12

Whee! **I** is for **ice**.

Ii

And **inchworms**
and **iguanas**.
Praise God for
the **I** things.

Jj

J is for **jungles**.

And **juice**
and **jam**
and **jellybeans**
and **June**.
Praise God for
the **J** things.

K is for **kangaroos**.

And **koalas**
and **kitchens**
and **kids** in **Kenya**.
Praise God for
the **K** things.

Ll

L is for **lambs** and **lilies**.

And **lollipops** to **lick** and **lovely** things to **look** at. Praise God for the **L** things.

16

M is for **mothers** and **money** and **mice**.

Mm

And **musical**
monkeys
and the **man**
in the **moon**.
Praise God for
the **M** things.

17

Nn

N is for **noses** and **nuts** and **noon**.

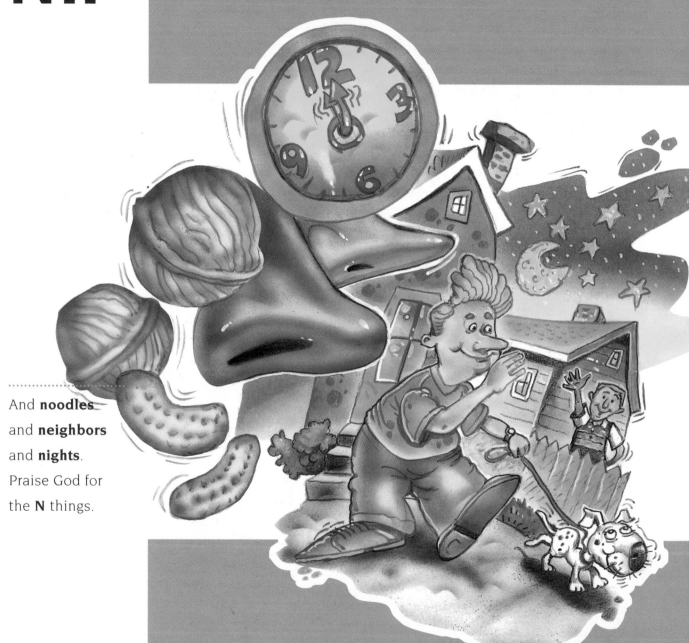

And **noodles** and **neighbors** and **nights**. Praise God for the **N** things.

O is for **OH!** An **opossum!**

Oo

God made **olives** and **oranges** and **octopi** too. Praise God for the **O** things.

Pp

P is for **pigs** in a **puddle**.

And **poodles**
and **popcorn**
and **pinecones**
in snow.
Praise God for
the **P** things.

Q is for **queens.**

Qq

And **queues** of **quail quietly** doing a **quickstep**. Praise God for the **Q** things.

21

Rr

R is for **roads** and **rabbits** and **ribbits** from frogs.

And **rivers**
and **robins**
and **rainbows**
to follow the **rain**.
Praise God for
the **R** things.

S is for the **sun** and the **snails**.

Ss

And **Sundays** and **sunflowers** and **snuggles** and **sleep**. Praise God for the **S** things.

Tt

T is for **turtles.**

And **tall trees** and **tomorrow** and **time** with each other. Praise God for the **T** things.

U is for **uncles** and **umbrellas**.

Uu

And **umpteen** things in the **universe** whose **uses** we don't yet **understand**. Praise God for the **U** things.

25

Vv

V is for **violets**.

And **vacations** and **visitors** and **vanilla** ice cream. Praise God for the **V** things.

W is for **water**. **Ww**

Wonderful,
wet water,
wiggly worms,
and **watermelons**.
Praise God for
the **W** things.

X x

X is for **X-rays.**

And **xylophones** too. But not many other things start with X. Praise God for the **X** things.

Y is for **yaks**.

Yy

And **yawns**
and **yogurt**.
And God
made **YOU**.
Praise God for
the **Y** things.
And praise
God for **you**!

Zz

Z is for **zooming zebras.**

God made
the **zebras**
and **zinnias**
and **zephyrs**
(those are breezes).
Praise God for
the **Z** things.

God made things from **A** to **Z**.

A–Z

And everything God made is good. So let's praise God from **A** to **Z**.

Dear Parent/Teacher:

This little book is packed with lots of learning activities for your children. First read the book to them all the way through. Let them study those things hidden in each picture that begin with the letter mentioned.

Then let them read the book to you, using only the top line on each page. Next you can take turns, the children reading the top lines and you reading the bottom lines. It won't be long before they can read the whole book alone!

Of course, the most important lesson in the book is that of God's unchanging love for the children, especially in a world full of things God made from A to Z.

 *The Editor*